WHISPER TO THE EARTH

ALSO BY DAVID IGNATOW

WHISPER TO THE EARTH

New Poems by

DAVID IGNATOW

An Atlantic Monthly Press Book
LITTLE, BROWN AND COMPANY
BOSTON / TORONTO

FIRST EDITION

Many of the poems in this collection have previously appeared, in
Arion's Dolphin, boundary 2 ("Growing Up," under the title
"I'm a Boy"), *Chicago Review, The Georgia Review* ("To Oneself,"
"In the Garden"), *Gravida, The Hampden-Sydney Poetry Review,
Harper's Magazine, Intrepid, Kayak, Kenyon Review* ("With Horace"),
Lillabulero, Little Caesar, Madrona, Moons and Tailes, The Nation
("Kaddish," "1905"), *New Letters* ("Thus Truly"; "Company," under
the title "In This Poem I Am a Cripple"; "Of That Fire"; "The Window";
"Street Scene"; "I Am"; "Behind His Eyes"; "A Requiem"),
News of the Universe, Next, The Niagara Magazine ("Father and Son"),
*The North Stone Review, Ontario Review, Paris Review, Pequod,
Plainsong, Poetry Magazine* ("I Love to Fly"; "The Ship," under the title
"Live It Through"; "A Cloud Creates"), *The Poetry Miscellany,
Poetry Now, Portland Review Magazine, Quest/80, Sun,* and
Unmuzzled Ox ("On Censorship," "On Freedom").

Library of Congress Cataloging in Publication Data

Ignatow, David, 1914-
  Whisper to the earth.

  "An Atlantic Monthly Press book."
  I. Title.
PS3517.G53W5   811'.54   81-8258
ISBN 0-316-41494-8   AACR2

ATLANTIC–LITTLE, BROWN BOOKS
ARE PUBLISHED BY
LITTLE, BROWN AND COMPANY
IN ASSOCIATION WITH
THE ATLANTIC MONTHLY PRESS

BP

Designed by Janis Capone

*Published simultaneously in Canada
by Little, Brown & Company (Canada) Limited*

PRINTED IN THE UNITED STATES OF AMERICA

TO THE MEMORY OF JAMES WRIGHT

CONTENTS

❧

ONE

TWO

THREE

FOUR

(Four Conversations)

FIVE

ONE

As I view the leaf, my theme is not the shades of meaning that the mind conveys of it but my desire to make the leaf speak to tell me, Chlorophyll, chlorophyll, breathlessly. I would rejoice with it and, in turn, would reply, Blood, and the leaf would nod. Having spoken to each other, we would find our topics inexhaustible and imagine, as I grow old and the leaf begins to fade and turn brown, the thought of being buried in the ground would become so familiar to me, so thoroughly known through conversation with the leaf, that my walk among the trees after completing this poem would be like entering my own house.

This time I can't grieve
over their deaths in yellow and wine red.
The tree bark is light gray
and a blue jay has just swooped in
to land on a branch, shaking leaves
loose. They do a dance on the air
as they fall.

A man has been tied to a tree and thinks he is beginning to feel something of the tree enter his body. It is hard for him to discern what it could be, but he would like to grow tiny branches from his head, and leaf buds.

He loves standing still. He thinks he can feel the tree pressing up against him, as if it were trying to instill in him its nature and its seed. He is in a kind of trance about himself. Thinking, as he had sensed before, is no longer a function of thought but of action. That is because he has welcomed the possibility of tiny branches and leaves that now he believes are growing from his sides and from his head. He would laugh in pleasure but that he finds himself swaying back and forth as in a dance that could have been induced by wind.

He is very happy, very much the tree, and he has shed his alarm at having been tied to it in the middle of the woods and left to die. He can forget the reason for his captivity which he thinks of no longer as capture but as a piece of luck to have happened in the midst of this crisis in his life. He is free of crisis, and can celebrate by bringing forth more branches and leaves, and he straightens up from his now stooped posture of exhaustion to let new growth emerge more easily from his head and sides. He is alive and that is what counts, alive in a form he has always admired, and now it is his and he is glad, only to find himself growing more sharply stooped and losing memory of himself, as this last thought becomes the bark he has seen behind his eyes.

Looking out on it from my window
I feel contiguous with it,
perhaps by our common air
and that we are in each other's presence.
Here, as proof, is this thought,
this one the most intriguing,
for in one leap I stand outside my self,
seeing myself from a tree's standpoint,
and I do look peculiar
moving about.

A cloud creates the face of a man who, happening to look up, recognizes it as his own. The face under stress of the wind begins to disintegrate into wings, and the man sees in himself the ability to fly. He stretches forth his arms and waves them up and down as he begins to circle and dip as a birdman would in the currents of the wind, and then the face vanishes and the wings drift apart, too, in shreds and patches.

The clouds darken, as they will; thunder rolls from their colliding with each other. Lightning flashes. He knows he is at war with himself, the reason for which he cannot go into at the moment.

There is no consolation, not until the rain ceases and the sun emerges and once more clouds arrive, white, brilliantly lit, and so for him full of hope. He has not attempted to sort out his, as it seems, random feelings since sighting the face. And though there is no order to his feelings, of that he is certain, he needs none, not while the sun rises and sets and weather prevails. It is from weather that he derives, and so he has no faults. He is without fault, he is of the weather.

Admit the sky carries no threatening message
in cloud or color. The birds wing by,
your only disturbance and pleasure. The grass
gives you gentleness and the earth selflessness.
You are encouraged on all sides by the impersonal.
Admit: the grasshopper sways upon a blade of grass,
men rest themselves upon the flood.

I am of the family of the universe, and with all of us together I do not fear being alone; I can reach out and touch a rock or a hand or dip my feet in water. Always there is some body close by, and when I speak I am answered by a plane's roar or the bird's whistling or the voices of others in conversation far apart from me. When I lie down to sleep, I am in the company of the dark and the stars.

Breathe to me, sheep in the meadow. Sun and moon, my father and my father's brother, kiss me on the brow with your light. My sister, earth, holds me up to be kissed. Sun and moon, I smile at you both and spread my arms in affection and lay myself down at full length for the earth to know I love it too and am never to be separated from it. In no way shall death part us.

I exist without the dignity of stone
that does not bother that it exists,
and so let me place my hand upon an open flame
and cry out my pain because I exist.
What other is there, without an open hand
into which the apple falls at end of autumn
or that cups the rain of a summer sky
or opens to the sun or moon? I am
the door to tomorrow.

A swordsman came charging out of his castle with sword unsheathed, wildly swinging at the air. He would slay air. It was the cause of his enemy's being alive. If he could not meet him to cut him down, at least he would destroy his enemy at the source, and he charged into the open meadow, thrusting, parrying, shouting execrations at air for ignoring him, for giving him to breathe too. But air was not to be killed by the sword, and so he rested. If there had to be enemies, then there had to be air also, or he too would die. He had to accept his enemy as he had to accept himself, as he had to accept air and water too. He was thirsty from effort, and there on the opposite side of the brook he saw his enemy stooping to drink. He waved at him good-naturedly. "Do you know we are part of nature and that it is as natural for us both to be enemies as it is natural for air to be and for us to breathe it in?" The enemy looked up from his drinking, released his short knife from its belt, and flung it with great force towards the opposite shore, where it plunged into the chest of the swordsman, to his surprise. He sank to his knees in horror, in disbelief, in anger and in sudden understanding that he had suffered the evidence of indifference in nature, and as he died he was glad that he could die free of anger, free of shame at his death.

The skin also wrinkles in old age,
the meat still sweet, if less plump,
and one eats it casually
out of the bowl
where it had been sitting
with other wrinkled fruit.

It's what the apple would want
if it could speak — to be enjoyed —
and one chews and enjoys
while chunk by chunk it vanishes
into the eater's mouth noisily
and is fulfilled.

The eternal men are deplaning at airports, briefcases under arm, arriving from a sales pitch or a conference on applications of scientific discoveries. They are sober with the experience of thinking, debating, deciding, and explaining, and are anxious to sit down at table to forget themselves in food and drink. They are tired and reluctant to state what life seems to them at this time. I am standing behind them, my face aglow, my body of light, and I am whispering of pleasure in my youthfulness: I have given up caring and thought. I am intoxicated with myself, and they are growing restless, hearing voices that arise in sleep when they are helpless. They turn on their seats to look into each other's faces, to study what is happening there, if anything like what they are hearing. I continue to whisper that I have penetrated their thoughts the way the sun penetrates a curtain at the window. I will light up their days and nights. I will make them restless for the balance of their days to go out and meet the sun as they travel in their hired cars and on their working flights to conferences. I am, and they are yet to become, yet to discover this in their sleep made brilliant by the sun of the memory of their youth.

And now I wish to pray and perform
a ritual of my devotion to the sun.
I will bow and sing beneath my breath,
then perform the dance of farewell
and my confidence in the sun's return.

All is dance: the sun glides along the horizon;
now the leaves sway;
now the earth spins.

Inside I am on fire. Imagine, though, running up to City Hall and asking if there is a Department of Burning Need,. ready for emergency, I being the emergency. I can see myself being locked up gently in a madhouse and declared as finished in this world of material evidence. Are my clothes on fire? Is my hair burning? Are my cheeks aflame? Do my feet scream with pain? My voice is calm and my clothes intact, my hair and face moist with sweat, and the oils of my body. Normal. "Where is the fire?" the cops ask sarcastically, giving me a ticket for speeding my brain beyond the legal limit and remanding me to court. I plead guilty and admit to it publicly, for I have no evidence but my spoken word, and all the while I know that the cop, the judge and the jury are burning within too, without a shred of evidence either. They'll laugh and shake their heads and signify with a twirl of their fingers at their heads a crazed man before them, which will show how sane they are, not knowing they are dying in the fire that was lit in them, born of that fire.

This is how I felt as a child:
I was high on self-delight
at the touch of the mild sun and breeze.
Here it is Spring again
and I have lost my sixty-fifth year
in the blinding sun.

🐦 I DREAM

I dream I am lying in the mud on my back and staring up into the sky. Which do I prefer, since I have the power to fly into the blue slate of air? It is summer. I decide quickly that by lying face up I have a view of the sky I could not get by flying in it, while I'd be missing the mud.

Each stone its shape
each shape its weight
each weight its value
in my garden as I dig them up
for Spring planting,
and I say, lifting one at a time,
There is a joy here
in being able to handle
so many meaningful
differences.

If trees that are lesser than I, so it is said by others, respond to Spring with an offering of leaves each season, can I do less than offer at least one poem in praise of breathing at regular intervals?

Looking out the window at the trees
and counting the leaves,
listening to a voice within
that tells me nothing is perfect
so why bother to try, I am thief
of my own time. When I die
I want it to be said that I wasted
hours in feeling absolutely useless
and enjoyed it, sensing my life
more strongly than when I worked at it.
Now I know myself from a stone
or a sledgehammer.

I identify with the wooden shed in my neighbor's backyard and with the cords of wood neatly piled. I am identified with the necessary, whether I myself am necessary. Why does a man go on breathing when he is in despair? How would it help to know, consciously, clearly, rationally, but what is rational about the necessary? If to live and have pride in oneself is rational, then the necessary is rational. I say to my neighbor, I hope you will have a warm fire from those cut logs and that your wooden shed will keep your tools clean and safe from dirt and frost, and I begin to feel myself bodily alive again, proud to have a body like any shed or cord of cut logs.

TWO

These were among my first thoughts on earth: I had been placed here as some kind of reward, given the gift of being what I was, and I loved my bike, praising it for moving at the command of my pedaling, and steering in the right direction at my touch. The sidewalk lay flat and still, expecting the bike. It, too, cooperated with the powers that be, and no one stood in the bike's path to topple me over. The wind upon my face was like the hand of approval. Where then was my change hiding, my hidden change?

I never thought the bike betrayed me, nor the sidewalk, nor the wind, but now I see them simply as means, and the betrayer is me. I cannot call the bike an emissary. It is a tool, the sidewalk a path, the wind a current of air. We are no longer communicating that I'm aware of, but what does it matter, I tell myself, so long as I am free to use all these for my delight; but I am alone in my pleasures. I am not the child of anyone, for, as I watch myself growing up, the bike shrinks in size and the sidewalk fills with cracks and bumps; the wind on my face in cold weather chills me, and when I eat I know it is because of appetite.

I have become something else, no longer at one with bike, sidewalk and wind. I can feel cold, hunger, appetite, the self and all that this means — because the bike never is hungry, nor does the sidewalk ever have to go to bed, and sometimes the wind stops blowing and for me does not exist, which, earlier, would have frightened me about myself, while the wind never is frightened; it never speaks about itself, as I am beginning to speak about myself, and so I know there is something about me very different. Sometimes I am panicky about it, but more often I am glad because I have still another thing to turn to in pleasure, and that is this self which is always with me, but I am alone because a tree has begun to look lonely to me standing by itself, whereas once I had thought it beautiful, saying what I felt about myself too — that I was, that we both were. Now the tree looks lonely, but I know that that also is my thinking, and the thinking is my pleasure and my burden too. I am all alone, and so I turn to another like myself and find him happy to turn to me.

And now we have begun to differ about the games we should be playing or the places to visit on our bikes or the time to go home for dinner. I become lonely again, my self needing to be defended as my only absolute friend and sharer, but my friend and I exchange smiles often and talk together with gentleness and teasing and wait for the voices of our parents to call us separately to dinner.

Ah, room, you wait for me day and night
faithfully silent expecting no reward
and if I do place a picture on your wall
you become so beautiful to look at
that it is I who am rewarded by your beauty.

You are so selfless, it is hard
for me to leave and visit other
and stranger rooms where I am not
as comfortable as I am with you
though they are fancier and even more
imposing with furniture and lamps
and it is for that reason that I am
not at ease as I sit there thinking
of you with bare floors and mostly
bare walls, undraped windows
like huge solemn eyes to look out
on the busy world. I long to return
to you in the midst of luxury and laughter
in ornate rooms. With you I can indulge
myself in sadness and in loss and feel
your self neutral in my presence
and ever willing to accept my thoughts
aloud, tears, my frantic phone calls
for a voice to speak back to me
in my loneliness with you. You do not
protest, you are not shocked, you are not
unhappy with me as perhaps you would be
in rooms so much more appointed and decorous,
where smiles and graceful gestures
and good witty talk are in order.
You do not harbor a grudge for your poverty
of chairs and tables, carpets and silken drapes.

You wait only for me and I arrive
almost anytime, even in the early hours
of the morning, yet you receive me
silently, openly.

If that is love then I am grateful,
and, if my feelings towards you
partake of that sense, then I am
a happy man. So together may we
last through other nights and days.
I will play you music on the radio
or turn on the TV for your pleasure.
Together we will view and hear
the world as lovers do, from a distance
of exalted ease in each other.

It was in an effort to be free from brick walls and it succeeded; but I do not see a face behind that window. Still, it is a window that offers hope of another face, and from time to time when I remember, I show myself at my window, in case someone is standing behind the curtain who needs the courage to show himself or herself that by standing in the light I can supply.

🐦 SOLITUDE

I am sitting here alone because it is important
to overcome, as catastrophe, sitting alone.
I believe it is just as good as being seated
in a crowd, and I would prove it by being seated
with my sense of togetherness with others
so that I may write of being alone
in a communal sense.

I am looking around for an exit from my loneliness that is like the vast, open, flat land of Kansas, gray sky, flecks of blue showing here and there. How do I find an exit from an untracked land? But a voice within, my voice, of course, keeps urging me to start walking. Which way? In any direction, the voice answers, and so I pick myself up from the ground where I had been sitting cross-legged, thinking, and begin to walk. I pass snake and badger holes. These animals live alone. I keep walking, there's no end to the horizon, nothing there to greet me that would take me out of myself, but to walk has become an activity. I am sad, but I can act.

One leaf left on a branch
and not a sound of sadness
or despair. One leaf left
on a branch and no unhappiness.
One leaf all by itself
in the air and it does not speak
of loneliness or death.
One leaf and it spends itself
in swaying mildly in the breeze.

I am a cripple, with my two arms hanging down over my head from the elbows. I have to walk that way, as if they were partially raised in despair with things as they are. But to have to walk through the streets with my arms raised above my head brings me the stares of strangers passing by. What could they think except that I am one of the many mad that walk freely through the streets, or a prophetic figure, which sets them to tremble inwardly, just after having received their latest bribe or their most recent prostitute. I suppose I could be some sort of message that allows me to walk through the streets with a show of confidence. But, when I am alone in my room, what then? I look in the mirror and frighten myself with my forearms dangling over my head, and I become severely depressed. Is this my fate from now on, I ask, to have my arms above my head in a gesture that could mean total despair? I am alone, and so I rush out again to find people with whom to mingle in the street to share my misfortune. And should you be one of those who does get to see me walking with my two arms dangling above my head from the elbows down, I live to receive your stares of sympathy, awe, terror or hate. I do not pass judgment on you, and if you should find it in yourself to see me as but a human being in trouble, think of me as company too.

I assume a Buddha-like expression in the mirror.
All that is needed now is to remove the doubt
lingering in my eyes, staring back at me
with amusement. It could be the Buddha,
all comprehending, entertained
to see me wish for that
which already should have been.

And so I am not he, nor can ever attain
to his role, but that he could shine
out of my eyes in the mirror tells me
he exists because I wish for that
which, as Buddha, I should have become.

I am, and so Buddha and I are not one,
but this is for my human self
to know he exists and that I exist
in his eyes and am understood.

I'm sure trees are depressed also; they are so silent except when the wind blows, but notice how abundantly they grow their leaves and how tall they manage to become, thick around the waist like wrestlers. They wrestle with the wind. I could learn from them, and their leaves rattle and hiss among themselves as if leaves are grown to express depression. But see how thickly they grow upon the branch and what shade they give to persons passing or seated beneath. It's an odd function for a depressed tree. I was about to try a razor on my wrist.

I am lying face up on a raft
floating upon a lake. The waves
are small, rocking me gently.
I am myself, in love with ease,
my arms and legs loose, my breathing
so low I study my being alive.
And at last, invigorated by my ease,
I turn, cup my head in hand
supported by an elbow against the raft,
and search the woods and waters
for a friend or stranger
with whom to share my self.

You wait in a rocking raft
or lie close against the ground
like its lover.

Once upon a time a man stole a wolf from among its pack and said to the wolf, "Stop, you're snapping at my fingers," and the wolf replied, "I'm hungry. What have you got to eat?" And the man replied, "Chopped liver and sour cream." The wolf said, "I'll take sour cream. I remember having it once before at Aunt Millie's. May I bare my teeth in pleasure?" And the man replied, "Of course, if you'll come along quietly," and the wolf asked, "What do you think I am? Just because I like sour cream you expect me to change character?" The man thought about this. After all, what was he doing, stealing a wolf from its kind, as if he were innocent of wrongdoing? And he let the wolf go but later was sorry; he missed talking to the wolf and went in search of it, but the pack kept running away each time he came close. He kept chasing and the pack kept running away. It was a kind of relationship.

My father, listening to music, that's me,
my legs outstretched upon the bed
as I lean back in my chair. I think of him
in his chair, legs crossed carelessly
and with his musing smile recalling his first wish,
to become a baritone, his smile seeking
after his youth or watching it in the distant past,
untouchable. I am alone, and the opera playing
heightens my loneliness, without son, without father,
without past or present, and my future a problem.

Eh, father, as I listen to your favorite opera
you would have enjoyed my listening and approved
emphatically, while I'd withhold myself,
tentative towards opera, as other matters burned in me,
such as the need to be free,
and so we would argue but soon fall silent
and go our separate ways.

I am alone in my apartment, alone as you were
without me in your last days at about my age.
I am listening to Rossini and thinking of you
affectionately, longing for your presence once more,
of course to wrestle with your character,
the game once again of independence,
but now, now in good humor
because we already know the outcome,
for I am sixty-six, going on sixty-seven,
and you are forever seventy-two.
We are both old men and soon enough
I'll join you. So why quarrel again,
as if two old men could possibly settle
between them what was impossible
to settle in their early days?

I have become friendly with baby cockroaches that dare to come out in the daylight to see what am I cooking or peeling. They're like little children curious about their elders and would like to know. I watch them scurry about on their invisible legs, they are so gentle and enquiring and frightened. When I raise my hand or lower a spoon they race off to a crack in the stove fixtures. Occasionally I crush one with my thumb on an impulse and go back to my cooking or peeling potatoes.

As for their parents, long as the first joint of my thumb, when I turn on the light at night I watch them in anger. I begin to spray with a poison. That their deaths will diminish the birth rate of their children does not bother me. It's the horror of their aggressive search for food that I react to viciously.

I leave the kitchen with its noxious poisonous smell and forget about their struggling death to listen to my radio, to read my book, to do my schoolwork, to think of how empty is my apartment with just myself in it, sick of being alone, always alone and not knowing how to change it to a life of friends.

While my father walked through mud
in shoes borrowed from his sister,
all Kiev attended *Prince Igor* and cheered,
and while he worked in a cellar bindery
and slept on workbenches rats leapt over
at night, Dostoyevsky's *White Nights*
and *Anna Karenina* were being read avidly
amid joy, tears and protests. My father
was the silent one, walking through the streets
where the hot arguments went on about poverty
and guilt. He walked, his work bundle under arm,
from cellar to monastery, to bind holy books
and volumes of the Russian classics,
and when they had had enough of classics
and needed blood, he fled,
for his blood was real to them; only he
had worked and starved. All others were
but characters in a novel or a play,
bless Chekhov, Gogol and others for their genius,
but my father was the one who had not been
immortalized and made untouchable.
Only he was real in Russia's torment.
Only he stood for life. All else was books,
and that was the torment.

The sounds of labor in the street, hammers at work to open pavement, ignore me. Everything is itself and so must return to itself after the event towards which it travels, as does the hammer that strikes at the pavement repeatedly but takes on nothing of its grayness or concrete strength. One resists while the other insists, and there is no meeting of qualities that each could appreciate and want to share.

I am striking at myself to open and plant a tree or make room for my friend who then I could say was a close, loving companion, going with me wherever I must go. This is what it means to be alone.

What keeps me intact after each strike is to know that my face has taken on the shape of each blow, and when I meet with others we measure our suffering at a glance. In deepest secret we are each other's subject of pain, thus truly as one.

❧ PREPARING

I'll have to see my father dead
and I just know
that I do certain things
to live. Beyond that
are wordless men
doing the work they have to:
murder is one
and loving is another.

I am alone with life, and we do not talk to each other, as if life were waiting for me to come to an end of my performance of itself. It stands by silently and aloof, leaving me to fend for myself.

I would guess that this is all life has to offer, and yet it must offer itself to become, and so I am the life it is.

I am wondering, but life is not. I am asking questions of it, but life is not, as if it has enough to do handing itself from person to person to keep itself alive; and now I'm receiving it.

Is it possible life is unhappy with itself? It does not speak except as I speak, and does not act except as I act. It has no independence other than what I do for myself. It is a puppet of its own making and allows me to be the one to manipulate the strings.

I am life, then, in fact; and I am the one who should speak to me. There is no one else, even if I were to speak to friends. We would be speaking to mirrors, and so I can deny or reject myself or make do and make merry with myself. I can do each on alternate days, not to neglect any one choice, since as life I must be as life, impersonal in my choices. I am happy indeed with this discovery, a discovery it is. I am a life of wonder at myself.

Mother of my birth, for how long were we together
in your love and my adoration of your self?
For the shadow of a moment, as I breathed your pain
and you breathed my suffering. As we knew
of shadows in lit rooms that would swallow the light.

Your face beneath the oxygen tent was alive
but your eyes closed, your breathing hoarse.
Your sleep was with death. I was alone
with you as when I was young
but now only alone, not with you,
to become alone forever, as I was learning
watching you become alone.

Earth now is your mother, as you were mine, my earth,
my sustenance and my strength,
and now without you I turn to your mother
and seek from her that I may meet you again
in rock and stone. Whisper to the stone,
I love you. Whisper to the rock, I found you.
Whisper to the earth, Mother, I have found her,
and I am safe and always have been.

I saw an ocean liner in the desert, its crew leaning over the railing, as though the ship were plowing through the waves of sand. I was reluctant to ask how a ship came to rest in the desert. The world itself was strange enough, and I did not want to ask questions that would make matters worse. I hailed the crew from my position on the sand and asked where the ship was headed and was answered promptly, Into the desert. I asked to come on board and at once a rope ladder was handed down. I climbed eagerly; we would go through with this absurdity together since, after all, it was our experience, and we could help each other to live it through.

Mother, in my unwanted suffering,
I turn to you who knew suffering
like an odor of food and breathed it in
with that familiarity. I can learn
from you to become my self, eating my sorrow
with my bread and gazing frankly at the world
as a man, as you, a woman, taught me
by your silence and acceptance of sorrow,
the bread itself.

A black man is hugging me around the throat from behind with his forearm as he demands in a rapid undertone my money. I think of his embrace as nearly an affectionate one, as if from a son who has come up from behind to demand his stipend for the week in a playful imitation of a mugger. I turn carefully as I would to a son for whom I have the greatest affection and say gently, "The money is in my breast pocket," and I make a motion towards it with my hand. He strikes my hand, as if carrying on the game of mugger, in case, as in the game, I was reaching for a gun. I say again gently to my black son, "The wallet is in my breast pocket." He does not smile. He lets me reach into my jacket to bring forth the wallet, which I do, and he snatches it from me. The game between us has become serious. I am in danger, but I react with calm.

Is this my son, this tall, husky young man who is extracting the bills from the fold and now returning the wallet? I am cautious. I did not train him to be a killer nor threatener, but he is serious about the money, and he pockets it all. I have an empty wallet that I return automatically to my breast pocket. He and I look at each other. I think I have a smile on my face, and I think he sees it and is mildly astonished, and maybe understands it or is curious to see a smile. We look at each other for another moment. There is curiosity between us. This is not my son but another man's, and he is acting towards me as a stranger. We are strangers, but we are to each other in the relationship of father and son by age. He opens the door to the elevator and orders me in. Will he kill me in the elevator? I look into his face; he must realize what I am thinking. He holds open the door, waiting for me to enter, not threatening me, simply waiting, and I enter. The door closes behind me. I look through the porthole to see him looking back at me.

Is he taking a last look at the man who could be his father whom he has subjugated to his will? I think I am still smiling. I think he is smiling back as the elevator begins to climb.

THREE

I am studying the hairs from my head that I was able to pull out gently this morning, as I do each morning instead of combing. Gray hairs, white hairs. I'm not convinced that I am old and that I should resign myself to finishing my days in quiet and calm. I continue to tug at the hairs in my balding head to find those that are firmly fixed in my scalp.

I wished for death often
but now that I am at its door
I have changed my mind about the world.
It should go on; it is beautiful,
even as a dream, filled with water and seed,
plants and animals, others like myself,
ships and buildings and messages
filling the air — a beauty,
if ever I have seen one.
In the next world, should I remember
this one, I will praise it
above everything.

In a clay pit he sees himself trying to climb out, the clay clinging to his feet keeping him down. He's puzzled, not very anxious, doesn't seem to be suffering from hunger or worry about dying in the pit. Just wondering whether he'll be able to get out. He tries again, fails; his feet can't detach themselves from that gray mass avalanching beneath the step that he takes to mount one side of the pit, and now finally the clay has buried his feet, and yet he wonders how it is that the clay supports him in his upright position.

That's it, to stand still, as he is forced to, and spend his time looking about at the sloping walls and on the natural designs of their uneven surfaces. And for how long will he stay here, he asks himself vaguely, as he concentrates on the walls. He has no answer, his question muted by his study of the walls.

because roads lead to towns
and do not generally end up in marshes
or deserts and because there are men
in session. Each morning they comb their hair
before the glass that shows the fine vapor
of their existence; they sit in chambers
for its exact word, neither sullen
nor filled with despair: dust too
must be as dust underfoot or on table
each morning wiped with a cloth clean.

This body on which I counted for an eternal life, this body with which I strolled out into the street to glory in the breeze of a summer sky, this body that will make me to lie down among the dead, that will close my eyes and close down its heart — how a body can do this to itself, having loved its own pleasures, enjoyed its own excitements, having sought after new ones every day. Yet it is ending itself too and I am caught in the middle, asking, Why can it not be consistent with its own love of its pleasures and go on, go on? I stare at it in the mirror and I look down on it naked and see nothing to have warned me in the past of its decision to be finished at a certain time, the legs sturdy, the thighs muscular, the stomach flat and hard.

It has stood in the fields at night to look up at the stars and count itself among them proudly as a body too glowing within, radiating its pleasure in being alive, to which others were attracted to make a pact of friendship and identity — this body intends to end itself in the ground beneath a pile of dirt. It will not listen to my pleas, to its own pleas, as I hear them repeated within me and echoing in my brain. It expects to die. It does not know whether it wants to die but I do know it intends to die, as if it were obediently following instructions like a soldier on the firing line who sees the prisoner, his best friend, tied to the stake but who is waiting for the order to fire. He will fire, he will grieve in silence, he will repress his grief, he will forget his friend.

(Al Lichtman)

He stood with two-wheeler between us,
cuffs pinned by clips
to keep from tearing on the sprocket;
I looked away. In the house we had sat
seeking each other's pattern
with feeble lights: words about the weather.
We had lit ourselves, fixed in perpetuity —
he rounded, easy to start, hard to stop;
I, rough all over, bogged down in my rudeness.
He had talked as if it were a plan for paradise.
I sat stolidly, like an egg flattened
on its bottom.

    He arose, sensing the loneliness
made with one's private eyes; and I, conceding that,
arose to say good-by. With a two-wheeler between us,
he let me feel where I had failed him,
his brown eyes vacant.

     . . .

Death has given him what he had sought,
a perfect amiability with life,
all other friendships failing.

If you look closely at the exhalations of my inner heat distorting the air around me, you will see I am burning; my eyes shine, my skin glows, I move legs, arms, head and body restlessly as fire. Have I burned others? I can assume I have. Have I been burned in return? That's when I burn brighter.

My flesh one day will have shriveled towards my bones, my bones turned brittle, my mind shrunk to silence, my spirit low as ashes. Ending in my own fire, I will have resolved myself into an image: "I live for you, I burn for you, I burn my self. Keep alive, and when nothing else helps, close your eyes, pretend you are asleep."

I trembled when I heard the news.
Who else must go, I finally asked myself,
to prove the world is temporary.

Good-by, young man. In your grave
I want you comforted in your silence
that this old age is but the absence
of youth.

Very much alike is our condition,
except that I must feel it
all the short days that are left to me.

We traversed the distance between us
on the bridge of our smiles. You saw me
as old and kind, and you I saw as understanding
my wish to be kind, not to talk
of growth and decay, my life simplified
by its coming death, but you went before me,
and now that you have led the way,
I may follow without fear,
your gift to me.

I am seated on a chair resting upon a wooden floor supported by a concrete foundation poured and sealed into the earth that whirls in space without visible support. I am quite worried. This whirling sphere does not know its own future nor its past, and is traveling at a reckless speed into the dark. I hold my breath, expecting to crash at any moment with a star or comet, but I can't hold my breath for long, and I begin to breathe in trepidation.

And here I thought I could take pride in my ancestral beginnings, the history of my tribe, their complications, their rise and fall, as if they had been the real beginning. My lordly Indian killers, god keepers, makers of cloth and slave runners, all who endured their life's darkness are traveling with me in the dark in their respected graves.

Now the steam hammer is still
on Easter Sunday, and the steel girders
are lined up alongside each other
like witnesses of their own lives.
Tomorrow they will begin their descent
into the ground like gods
who need to be buried in ceremony
so that all can witness and say amen.

I'm alive only to prove the existence of death in me too,
I'm alive only to make death visible to myself and to others,
and I think that to be alive with these thoughts
is to be experiencing death at the same time.

I go from one thought to the other as in a walk
from the dark side to the sunlit and back to dark
when the sun grows too hot for my uncovered head —
uncovered in honor of the sun, when as it starts to burn
my scalp I know it is time to move across the street
and into shade. I walk until I tire of the cool,
once more longing for the sun, as I gaze
upon its brilliant pleasure in itself.

I commute between two worlds
and expect to succumb in time to one or the other,
for if I linger in the sun too long
the shade will come upon me from within
and if I walk in shade I will grow cool as death,
but having walked in both shade and sun
I will have lived forever
in seeing nothing change but variations
in the change from shade to sun.

I saw a leaf flying in the opposite direction from the ground, but there was no wind. Now how could that be, I asked myself. It was a dead leaf, shriveled and brittle looking, one of the many hundreds that were dropping to the ground off the trees beside my house. Puzzled for an explanation, thinking perhaps an updraft had caught the leaf and sailed it into the sky, I watched it grow smaller and smaller to the eye, and soon I could not make it out at all. I shrugged and entered my house and closed the door behind me. I could imagine the house beginning to take off too, and I sat down as if to pin it to the ground, when, as I seated myself, there was a tapping on the door. I was expecting company. I approached and opened the door. A single leaf lay on the doorstep at my feet.

If there is anything else to life besides living it
we would know, wouldn't we, by something
going on inside, like a loud hum of urgency
or an illumination of our insides day and night?
But since we just sit or eat and then go
to the toilet or make love and get dressed,
are you disappointed? Do you wish to rebel?
Will you write out a protest?
And I wish I knew what I could say.
I also am sad and so write it out
and leave it all behind for others
to give it thought that will make a bond
between the living and the dead.

FOUR

(Four Conversations)

Do I feel a moral outrage about immoral acts? No.
Am I a friend of the people? No.
Do I believe in justice and mercy? No.
Do I have a love for others? No.

Do I have a love for myself? No.
Do I live out of love for the world? No.
Am I a happy man? No.
Am I desirous of the happiness of others? No.
Do I look forward to a future of peace and plenty for the
    world? No.
Do I contemplate the destruction of the world? Yes.
Do I hope for it? No.

Am I looking forward to my own death? Yes.
Am I hoping for it? No.
Am I enjoying my life? Yes and No.
Is there anything I want to say before I die? No.
Do I feel satisfied with what I have done in this life? No.
Do I expect to see an improvement? No.
Is there a possibility in my mind that such an improvement
    can be made? No.
Doesn't that upset me and make me sad or depressed or want
    to get myself to do something about it? No.
How do I manage to live in this kind of pessimism?
    I contemplate it.

I always speak with the voice of God.

How's that?

Because he wants me to.

Do you mean he lends you his voice as he remains silent?

Exactly. Isn't he nice?

I should say. I wonder what he could do for me, if I asked?

What have you got on your mind?

I'd like his authority and power.

Well, why not ask him?

O.K., I will.

So ask.

Oh, do I ask you?

Yes, of course. I am the voice of God.

I see. Well, you're also human, so you're not going to give me the authority and power.

By no means.

Then why did you want me to ask?

So's I could say no and show you my authority and power.

I believe you.

Do you want me to demonstrate to you, anyhow?

Sure, go ahead.

O.K. Disappear!

Who?

You!

Me?

Yeh.

Disappear? What do you mean, disappear?

I mean disappear, vanish. Get lost.

By whose authority?

By mine.

Make me disappear.

But you don't understand. When I speak it's to be listened to and obeyed.

I see, the voice of God.

Exactly.

O.K., I'll tell you what I'm going to make disappear — my foot up your behind, I'm going to kick your ass so hard!

Don't you dare!

Why not?

Because I'll tell on you.

Oh, you will. Who'll you tell, voice of God?

I'll tell myself.

I see. And then what?

I'll get mad.

And then what?

I'll disappear.

You'll disappear?

Yes, I won't be around any longer.

You'll leave me.

Yes.

You'll take the voice of God with you.

And leave you alone, all by yourself, to worry and take care of yourself.

Is that so?

Yes, and you'll miss me and cry for me and have no one to turn to for help and advice and prayer.

I'll pray anyway.

But nobody will listen. There'll be nobody to hear you.

Oh yes, I'll hear myself and so will my neighbors, if I'm in a group.

And you'll be praying to nothing and nobody because I won't be there. I'm going.

Wait.

Why?

You're funny. Stick around.

And then what?

O.K., we'll pray to you and listen to your advice and laugh.

How's that?

O.K., laugh, but don't expect to get results.

O.K. We never did anyway. You're one of us.

Oh yeh? I'm the voice of God.

And so am I.

Why?

Because I feel like it. I feel like you.

Oh.

Yeah, now you pray to me and like it.

Pray to you? I'm the voice of God.

So am I.

So we're even.

O.K., we're even. We're walking, talking voices of God and we can communicate with one another. How's that?

Great.

We'll tell each other fabulous things.

We'll give each other great dreams and emotions and futures and we'll be happy in a dream.

Hey, man, we're making it together.

What do you know!

We're pleased.

We're content.

We're special.

We're peculiar.

Why?

Because I said so.

That ain't enough.

Well, you say it too and it'll be unanimous.

We're peculiar. We're ourselves. We're anybody we want to be. We're the voice of God. We have his authority and power. Because we say so.

Aren't you tired of this game?

Oh, is it a game? I didn't know.

Know any other?

I wait for the mailman.

Why do you wait for the mailman?

He gives me something to anticipate, the opening of letters, finding bills and reminders of sales and notes from friends to say hello and what are you doing and why don't you write or come for a visit or can he come to visit me or he may have something to say about a mutual friend divorced or remarried or a success in love or publishing. Something, that is what I am waiting for.

Well, may I wait with you, then?

Is there going to be mail for you too, in my batch?

No.

Then why wait?

It will be nice watching you open your letters. It's something to anticipate, as you say, and I would like to enjoy it along with you, or if that's too personal and intrusive I could stand at a distance and just watch your face as you read each letter.

Oh, then you watching me will add a new wrinkle, as I watch myself, a double perspective.

Right, and then I knowing you are watching me watching you will add yet a third perspective.

Exactly, and knowing that both of us will be watching each other will add yet another dimension.

Intensely?

Imaginatively?

Authentically?

With pleasure, pain, sorrow, joy, happiness, fear and dread, depending upon the letter.

And perhaps in satisfaction and fulfillment.

In consummation.

Hinting at a mystery.

In us.

And around us.

In awe.

In worship.

Godhead.

Paradise.

Hell?

Purgatory?

In letters?

They'll be coming from humans like ourselves, filled with their own needs and joys, pleasures, identities, dread, happiness, terror and awe.

At sending the letters?

Aren't we all together in this?

Giving each other love, hate, bills, friendship and gossip.

Giving each other a circle, a closed circle.

A mystery?

An awesome awareness of ourselves. We live in a circle.

As if we were living in millions of bodies and brains and always with the same image flashed back to us, the same thoughts and emotions.

Is this happiness?

Is this with dread and expectation, fear and joy, love and hate?

Is this the life in which we stand in awe?

Yearning for more of it, afraid to love, afraid to die.

Yearning for ourselves, more of ourselves, always more and more.

Always centered upon ourselves and emerging from ourselves to converge upon ourselves.

Renewed.

Refreshed.

Or hurt and sad.

Or killed outright.

By the hand of another man whom we know to be our self turning against us.

Divided from ourselves.

Bent on suicide.

What should we say to all this appalling commentary upon ourselves?

That it is us and we are living it and that we are the life we live and none other.

Do you have a solution?

We must think.

The letters have arrived. Here is the mailman.

Good morning, Mr. Mailman. We are very pleased to see you.

Thank you, but I get paid for doing this.

And we are grateful there is money with which to pay you.

Otherwise I would not be here.

Really.

I'd be out looking for another job.

And what about our letters?

Good-by, Mr. Mailman.

Did you see him shrug at my question?

And he did not even say good-by. Now I am sad.

And now perhaps we can make ourselves happier with the opening of these letters.

The better part of us.

We are turning ourselves around and around like a crystal chandelier, showing to ourselves all our lovely and unlovely parts.

Crystal chandeliers.

I'm looking for the idea of order.

Where are you looking for it?

Under the table.

How about the closet? Or under the bed? Or in the kitchen sink? Or in your pants pocket? Or in your wallet? Perhaps in your head?

I can't imagine finding it there.

Well, have you looked in the jails?

No, but I have looked in the bars.

How about the grocery stores? How about the banks? Or a garage?

Or a skating rink?

We'll find it, keep looking. You're not doing any harm.

And that's good?

What would you call it?

A kind of order.

An idea in search of its order? I know that in my mind I crave it.

And in my mind I miss it.

That's saying the same thing.

Of course, and I just remembered that there once was a woman with a very hairy face. I remember her from my childhood when I went with my father on a visit. I was struck dumb and all the way home later I could not say a word to my father as I kept thinking of this hairy face.

And that to you was a sign of disorder?

Yes, and I remember on a stroll with my father up the block we lived on passing a jewelry store with a man seated at the window repairing watches. I turned to my father and I said, I am going to become a watchmaker when I grow up. He smiled and said, Yes? And I nodded vigorously.

And that was a sign of order?

Yes.

Do you recall what happened to that hairy lady?

No. She was married to the house painter to whom we had gone to make arrangements to paint our house. He seemed not the least upset by his wife's appearance. And that felt like . . .

Order?

Yes.

So there was both order and disorder in that house?

I don't know whether that actually was the situation and I can't believe it can exist, given the same condition for both in the same place.

Then must we say that we don't know whether there was order or disorder or both?

Right.

And we don't have any solid answer to go on?

We're in the dark.

And all is as if back in a kind of first chaos.

Right.

And we have to live with it.

Right.

And make our peace with it in some kind of order.

A very tentative and problematical kind.

As for your ambition to become a watchmaker, did you become such a person?

It left my mind as soon as I became interested in something else.

And so you lost at least one idea of order through your own thinking and found yourself thinking of another kind of order.

I have forgotten what that one was.

FIVE

Two lovers with little to say to one another begin to quote from the headlines of the day's newspaper, and the excitement mounts from the front page through Sports and Finance, but when they come to Want Ads the sounds they emit to each other over the phone are simply indescribable. They have found their love again in its primal state, and as they are about to swoon with recovered ecstasy they turn a page and come upon the Obituary Column. They have much to grieve over, and grieve they do for each other's coming end and absence from this life, which will leave one lonely without the other.

Is there consolation for this loss of happiness and pleasure in each other? And, of course, their joy? They languidly turn the pages of the newspaper once again in their misery. It is an absentminded act, and they come upon ads for furniture, clothes, vacations, for the latest dance records and nightclubs, for the latest in styles, and they begin to glow, to think on life again. They can spend money, shop for a house, for a car to drive south in the winter; and furniture, a crib, attic space, a garden for vegetables and flowers — all as advertised in the newspaper. Two who could not be more happy, their love again spontaneous with pleasure in each other.

In a dream I'm no longer in love, I breathe deeply this sense of freedom and I vow never again to seal myself in, but I am reminded it is my self I love also and that too is a kind of sealed condition. I am committed to taking care of my body and its home accommodations, its clothes and neat appearance that I admire in the mirror. It is love and I would like to know what it would be like freed of brushing my teeth, washing my neck and face and between my toes. I'd like to know, as I neglect to move my bowels, and stay away from food that could sustain my health, and do not change my underwear, and let odors rise from my crotch and armpit. I stick out my tongue at the image in the mirror showing me my ragged beard and sunken eyes and hollow cheeks, free of my self-love at last, and I sink onto the bathroom floor, feeling life begin to seep out of me, I who haven't eaten since last month. I'm dying and I'm free.

But then I ask, having won the freedom to be dead, is that all? I struggle up on my feet and stagger over to the kitchen refrigerator and find an apple there nearly all rotten, and some moldy cheese. I eat, I'm free to eat.

A man, a famous man, is being talked about in another country and, because he is being talked about, an official from the Department of Culture has arrived at his house to strike him for each thought expressed by the stranger on this famous man. He asks, Why strike me when it's not I who is doing the talking? We strike you, the reply goes, because you are the surrogate for that man. When he stops talking about you, we will stop talking to you with our hands. The famous man decides to call up this stranger whose name he does not know and ask him or her to stop talking about him, and so he places the call with the operator, who says she knows exactly who the stranger is and that she is ready to call the person but first must strike herself over the head, as required by the rules of the Department of Culture. This she does and then proceeds to put through the call. The person answers the phone, listens, and gives one huge scream, which is heard by the famous man, who turns to the cultural attaché of his government and says, That person knows my work. I am delighted.

Dear fellow gull, a question or two for you to answer, if you care to. You're up there banking and floating in the wind. Is that for the pleasure of it or do you have something else in mind, such as spotting clams from that height? Secondly, as you walk along the shore, is that just for pleasure of walking or are you feeling with your feet for something to eat? The last question, what kind of soap do you use? We are advertising Cleano. Have you used it yet? Oh, you have and you say it tastes good? That's great. May we quote you? Thank you. There will be residuals from this: We'll be able to pay you for your endorsement of our product each time it flashes on the screen. We can send it to you in cash or in clams. You prefer clams? That'll be easy enough. We'll hire your fellow gulls to dig them out for you and provide them by the bushel. Oh, you don't want that? You've changed your mind? You want my bald head on which to drop your clams from a height. I can send you as many bald heads as you wish but you must excuse me if I withhold mine. You see, I'm program director and without me we can't get you on the screen with your commercial. You want me to resign and come live with you? I might try it someday but you must excuse me now, I must take your answers to the studio. You'd like to drop my head from a height and open it like a clam? (At this point, one hundred gulls are observed taking a good grip on the program director with their beaks and lifting him to the sky and releasing him in the air! He's still dropping. They catch him as he's about to land, fly him up into the air again, and release him; this time they mean to watch him land!)

In a dream I am making phone calls to dozens of airlines to find out the exact flight time to cities all over the world and enjoying the sounds of Amsterdam, Bangkok, San Francisco, Peking. I gloat at the thought of being in flight, seated luxuriously in my 747 and drinking vodka martinis, wines, liqueurs, soda pop, coffee, tea and malteds. I am many different kinds of persons, you see, because I cannot contain so much joy in myself alone. Finally, where do I want to go, these many different persons that I am? Mexico, Japan, England? Name the country, the city, the open field, the cliff, the mountain, the riverside, the ocean or the cave. I am confused; my many different persons make so many conflicting requests. I should go to Malaysia, but I hear my other selves sing Hong Kong, Ceylon, Indonesia, France, Africa. What do I do? It's not a matter of money. Sitting here and envisioning my trip doesn't cost a cent, but I want to go to one place at a time, explore it thoroughly, and move on from there. "Malaysia, please. Round trip to Malaysia." I am confounding all my other voices by deciding on Malaysia, and they are unhappy, which means I ultimately will be unhappy. Could I carry on a life like this, as, for example, loving one woman but hearing my voices suggest a dozen others all at once? This is madness. It certainly isn't middle class. What do I mean by dreaming all this? I should awaken and get rid of such temptations. I should awaken. All my other voices are in disagreement with me, and I love to fly.

I am the chair he sits on at the desk to type his poems and letters and comments on himself and others, a strange man. He can actually fart while typing the most soulful lines. I'm used to it and anyway what can I do to stop him or protest? I creak, I bend, I roll from beneath him and he promptly jerks me back towards the desk, a stern taskmaster.

What I'd like to do is write my own poem about him, but there I sit in front of the desk and typewriter in his absence and simply contemplate the idea. My two arms rest at my side and refuse to move upwards to the keys. What could I write about except about being a chair, previously a part of a tree trunk? Which was the better fate? I can hardly judge. My life is already fixed in its condition — to serve others — but I should take that as an omen of good. He does find me of value. Yet think of what will happen to me when he becomes too old to type! So we have something in common, don't we?

I wish he would recognize that and stop farting on me so that at least I could respect myself as he respects himself. Does he? We're equals in the end, aren't we? He should know that, being so smart as to know exactly what I'm thinking now, while he's typing my thoughts. I don't even have my private mind hidden from others, which shows you how much a slave I am. Does he have pity on me at all?

Oh, I do.

Now I hear two unsynchronized steel hammers pounding on steel, making contrapuntal sounds between them, as if to teach me the first simple lesson about order, that there are many kinds, and that two could cause discordancy between them as harsh as war; and now one hammer has stopped and it seems as if the other is pounding away even more rapidly to gain on the other if and when it starts again. I sit at my desk waiting for the answer, but now the silence is complete, the second hammer fallen silent, and I am left at my typewriter to make the necessary sounds that we associate with life.

With Horace I take my stand beside the rocks
and clear falls. I will not be confused
by sound or the stone's hardness. Voices
emerge from me and hardness takes from me
its quality, for Horace lived upon a mountainside
and made shapes that were not pliant.
He dug for rock, as I am of the born elements
compressed. Did he crush his wine grapes
underfoot? Did he mix with the rain
and the rivers? Who gave him grapes to grow?
Hard money. And am I sick, then, being happy?
He entered a stone house and struck off
his fire upon stone.